Baby Shower

_____

NAME

_____

DATE

_____

PLACE

 # Guests

NAME

_____

RELATIONSHIP TO THE PARENTS

_____

NOTE TO THE PARENTS

_____

_____

_____

WISHES FOR THE BABY

_____

_____

_____

Guests

NAME

_____

RELATIONSHIP TO THE PARENTS

_____

NOTE TO THE PARENTS

_____

_____

_____

WISHES FOR THE BABY

_____

_____

_____

 # Guests

NAME

_____

RELATIONSHIP TO THE PARENTS

_____

NOTE TO THE PARENTS

_____

_____

_____

WISHES FOR THE BABY

_____

_____

_____

 # Guests

NAME

RELATIONSHIP TO THE PARENTS

NOTE TO THE PARENTS

WISHES FOR THE BABY

 # Guests

NAME

RELATIONSHIP TO THE PARENTS

NOTE TO THE PARENTS

WISHES FOR THE BABY

Guests

NAME

_____

RELATIONSHIP TO THE PARENTS

_____

NOTE TO THE PARENTS

_____

_____

_____

WISHES FOR THE BABY

_____

_____

_____

Guests

NAME

_____

RELATIONSHIP TO THE PARENTS

_____

NOTE TO THE PARENTS

_____

_____

WISHES FOR THE BABY

_____

_____

Guests

NAME

_____

RELATIONSHIP TO THE PARENTS

_____

NOTE TO THE PARENTS

_____
_____
_____

WISHES FOR THE BABY

_____
_____
_____

 # Guests

NAME

_____

RELATIONSHIP TO THE PARENTS

_____

NOTE TO THE PARENTS

_____

_____

_____

WISHES FOR THE BABY

_____

_____

_____

Guests

NAME

_____

RELATIONSHIP TO THE PARENTS

_____

NOTE TO THE PARENTS

_____
_____
_____

WISHES FOR THE BABY

_____
_____
_____

 # *Guests*

NAME

_____

RELATIONSHIP TO THE PARENTS

_____

NOTE TO THE PARENTS

_____

_____

_____

WISHES FOR THE BABY

_____

_____

_____

 # Guests

NAME

_____

RELATIONSHIP TO THE PARENTS

_____

NOTE TO THE PARENTS

_____

_____

_____

WISHES FOR THE BABY

_____

_____

_____

 # Guests

NAME

_____

RELATIONSHIP TO THE PARENTS

_____

NOTE TO THE PARENTS

_____

_____

_____

WISHES FOR THE BABY

_____

_____

_____

 # Guests

NAME

_____

RELATIONSHIP TO THE PARENTS

_____

NOTE TO THE PARENTS

_____

_____

_____

WISHES FOR THE BABY

_____

_____

_____

 # Guests

NAME

_____

RELATIONSHIP TO THE PARENTS

_____

NOTE TO THE PARENTS

_____

_____

_____

WISHES FOR THE BABY

_____

_____

_____

 # Guests

NAME

_____

RELATIONSHIP TO THE PARENTS

_____

NOTE TO THE PARENTS

_____

_____

_____

WISHES FOR THE BABY

_____

_____

_____

Guests

NAME

_____

RELATIONSHIP TO THE PARENTS

_____

NOTE TO THE PARENTS

_____

_____

_____

WISHES FOR THE BABY

_____

_____

_____

 # *Guests*

NAME

RELATIONSHIP TO THE PARENTS

NOTE TO THE PARENTS

WISHES FOR THE BABY

Guests

NAME

_____

RELATIONSHIP TO THE PARENTS

_____

NOTE TO THE PARENTS

_____
_____
_____

WISHES FOR THE BABY

_____
_____
_____

 # *Guests*

NAME

_____

RELATIONSHIP TO THE PARENTS

_____

NOTE TO THE PARENTS

_____
_____
_____

WISHES FOR THE BABY

_____
_____
_____

Guests

NAME

_____

RELATIONSHIP TO THE PARENTS

_____

NOTE TO THE PARENTS

_____

_____

_____

WISHES FOR THE BABY

_____

_____

_____

 # Guests

NAME

RELATIONSHIP TO THE PARENTS

NOTE TO THE PARENTS

WISHES FOR THE BABY

# Guests

NAME

_____

RELATIONSHIP TO THE PARENTS

_____

NOTE TO THE PARENTS

_____

_____

_____

WISHES FOR THE BABY

_____

_____

_____

Guests

NAME

_____

RELATIONSHIP TO THE PARENTS

_____

NOTE TO THE PARENTS

_____

_____

_____

WISHES FOR THE BABY

_____

_____

_____

Guests

NAME

_____

RELATIONSHIP TO THE PARENTS

_____

NOTE TO THE PARENTS

_____

_____

_____

WISHES FOR THE BABY

_____

_____

_____

 # Guests

NAME

_____

RELATIONSHIP TO THE PARENTS

_____

NOTE TO THE PARENTS

_____

_____

_____

WISHES FOR THE BABY

_____

_____

_____

 # Guests

NAME

RELATIONSHIP TO THE PARENTS

NOTE TO THE PARENTS

WISHES FOR THE BABY

 # Guests

NAME

_____

RELATIONSHIP TO THE PARENTS

_____

NOTE TO THE PARENTS

_____

_____

WISHES FOR THE BABY

_____

_____

 # Guests

NAME

_____

RELATIONSHIP TO THE PARENTS

_____

NOTE TO THE PARENTS

_____

_____

_____

WISHES FOR THE BABY

_____

_____

_____

Guests

NAME

_____

RELATIONSHIP TO THE PARENTS

_____

NOTE TO THE PARENTS

_____

_____

_____

WISHES FOR THE BABY

_____

_____

_____

Guests

NAME

_____

RELATIONSHIP TO THE PARENTS

_____

NOTE TO THE PARENTS

_____

_____

WISHES FOR THE BABY

_____

_____

Guests

NAME

RELATIONSHIP TO THE PARENTS

NOTE TO THE PARENTS

WISHES FOR THE BABY

 # Guests

NAME

RELATIONSHIP TO THE PARENTS

NOTE TO THE PARENTS

WISHES FOR THE BABY

Guests

NAME

RELATIONSHIP TO THE PARENTS

NOTE TO THE PARENTS

WISHES FOR THE BABY

 # Guests

NAME

_____

RELATIONSHIP TO THE PARENTS

_____

NOTE TO THE PARENTS

_____

_____

WISHES FOR THE BABY

_____

_____

 # Guests

NAME

_____

RELATIONSHIP TO THE PARENTS

_____

NOTE TO THE PARENTS

_____

_____

_____

WISHES FOR THE BABY

_____

_____

_____

Guests

NAME

_____

RELATIONSHIP TO THE PARENTS

_____

NOTE TO THE PARENTS

_____
_____
_____

WISHES FOR THE BABY

_____
_____
_____

Guests

NAME

RELATIONSHIP TO THE PARENTS

NOTE TO THE PARENTS

WISHES FOR THE BABY

Guests

NAME

_____

RELATIONSHIP TO THE PARENTS

_____

NOTE TO THE PARENTS

_____

_____

_____

WISHES FOR THE BABY

_____

_____

_____

 # *Guests*

NAME

_____

RELATIONSHIP TO THE PARENTS

_____

NOTE TO THE PARENTS

_____

_____

_____

WISHES FOR THE BABY

_____

_____

_____

 # *Guests*

NAME

_____

RELATIONSHIP TO THE PARENTS

_____

NOTE TO THE PARENTS

_____

_____

_____

WISHES FOR THE BABY

_____

_____

_____

 # Guests

NAME

_____

RELATIONSHIP TO THE PARENTS

_____

NOTE TO THE PARENTS

_____

_____

_____

WISHES FOR THE BABY

_____

_____

_____

 # Guests

NAME

_____

RELATIONSHIP TO THE PARENTS

_____

NOTE TO THE PARENTS

_____
_____
_____

WISHES FOR THE BABY

_____
_____
_____

Guests

NAME

_____

RELATIONSHIP TO THE PARENTS

_____

NOTE TO THE PARENTS

_____

_____

_____

WISHES FOR THE BABY

_____

_____

_____

 # Guests

NAME

_____

RELATIONSHIP TO THE PARENTS

_____

NOTE TO THE PARENTS

_____

_____

_____

WISHES FOR THE BABY

_____

_____

_____

Guests

NAME

RELATIONSHIP TO THE PARENTS

NOTE TO THE PARENTS

WISHES FOR THE BABY

 # Guests

NAME

_____

RELATIONSHIP TO THE PARENTS

_____

NOTE TO THE PARENTS

_____

_____

_____

WISHES FOR THE BABY

_____

_____

_____

 # Guests

NAME

_____

RELATIONSHIP TO THE PARENTS

_____

NOTE TO THE PARENTS

_____

_____

_____

WISHES FOR THE BABY

_____

_____

_____

 # Guests

NAME

_____

RELATIONSHIP TO THE PARENTS

_____

NOTE TO THE PARENTS

_____

_____

_____

WISHES FOR THE BABY

_____

_____

_____

Guests

NAME

_____

RELATIONSHIP TO THE PARENTS

_____

NOTE TO THE PARENTS

_____

_____

_____

WISHES FOR THE BABY

_____

_____

Gift Log

NAME	GIFT	THANK YOU SENT?
_____	_____	☐
_____	_____	☐
_____	_____	☐
_____	_____	☐
_____	_____	☐
_____	_____	☐
_____	_____	☐
_____	_____	☐
_____	_____	☐
_____	_____	☐

Gift Log

NAME	GIFT	THANK YOU SENT?
_____	_____	☐
_____	_____	☐
_____	_____	☐
_____	_____	☐
_____	_____	☐
_____	_____	☐
_____	_____	☐
_____	_____	☐
_____	_____	☐
_____	_____	☐

Gift Log

NAME	GIFT	THANK YOU SENT?
		☐
		☐
		☐
		☐
		☐
		☐
		☐
		☐
		☐
		☐

Gift Log

NAME	GIFT	THANK YOU SENT?
		☐
		☐
		☐
		☐
		☐
		☐
		☐
		☐
		☐
		☐

Gift Log

NAME	GIFT	THANK YOU SENT?
		☐
		☐
		☐
		☐
		☐
		☐
		☐
		☐
		☐
		☐

Notes

Manufactured by Amazon.ca
Acheson, AB

13925272R00037